HIS CROWN
OF GLORY

HIS CROWN OF GLORY

The Old Rugged Cross

H G YEO

PARTRIDGE

A Penguin Random House Company

To order additional copies of this book, contact
Toll Free 800 101 2657 (Singapore)
Toll Free 1 800 81 7340 (Malaysia)
orders.singapore@partridgepublishing.com

www.partridgepublishing.com/singapore

Contents

Introduction

This book came about when the Holy Spirit brought to my mind a vision which I saw during one of my counselling sessions sometime back. As my counsellor and I were discussing about some specific issues in my life which needed healing, I saw Jesus coming into the room and gently draw out a broken part from my innermost being.

I recognised this broken part immediately. She had short hair and was wearing a long, black pants and white, long-sleeved shirt. She had been feeling miserable all her life, as she had carried a deep hatred in her heart towards her father. He had behaved as though he only had a son but not a daughter. I had earlier on, introduced this part to Jesus during one of my quiet moments, before going for counselling. She refused to listen to me. She said that "all men are the same." I told her that Jesus is different, that He longed to woo her, heal her, and take the place of her father who was never a father to her. She was adamant, so I told her to take some time to consider.

I watched as Jesus drew her to Him, embraced her in His arms, and then wrapped her with His left arm as they walked out of the room together. I sat speechless for a moment. My counsellor stared at me, and tried to draw my attention back to the session. I spoke slowly and told her what I just saw. She was equally speechless. As we pulled ourselves together to carry on with the session, I saw Jesus walked in again with the part. She looked different now. She had a radiance and glow about her, and she looked confident. Her attire had also changed. She wore a deep pink gown, and she had a Crown on her head. As she walked towards me, Jesus smiled, and turned and walked out of the room. I broke into tears.

The Holy Spirit told me to write about the five Crowns in the bible that believers in Jesus Christ will receive when our glorious Lord comes back again to reward us for our faith in Him. He also told me that Christians need to be constantly alert and aware of the devil and his wicked, evil exploits in going all the way out to destroy as many people as he can, especially so in this twenty-first century, because he knows that his time here on earth is getting shorter and shorter!

In chapter one, the Holy Spirit is challenging all Christians to get ready for the return of our Lord Jesus Christ. We can no longer be complacent in our Christian walk. We need to buck up because the signs of His imminent coming are there. Pre-believers will get the chance to receive their crown by following the sinner's prayer written for them. This chapter concludes with truths that Christians must establish in their hearts, souls and minds before going on to the next chapter.

Chapter two looks at each of the five crowns, as described in the bible by the apostles of Jesus Christ: 1) The Imperishable Crown, 2) The Crown of Rejoicing, 3) The Crown of Life, 4) The crown of Righteousness, and 5) The Crown of Glory.

In chapter three, we look at the need to recognise the spiritual forces of darkness we are battling with. We need to be aware of the devil's relentless destructive exploits to our hearts, souls, and minds. When we begin to understand why God made us in His image, we will stand up confidently as His Redeemed Children and drive the evil and wicked coward out of our lives for good! The Crown of Righteousness is ours when we walk tall as His Prince and Princess in the Righteousness of our Lord Jesus Christ! AMEN!

In chapter four, we expose the devil's strategies and plans to corrupt and defile our hearts, souls and minds against GOD. We plant the Word of God in our hearts, souls and minds so that we can use His Word as the tool, and the only tool, to counterattack against the wiles of the devil. The Imperishable Crown is ours when we keep our entire being from being defiled by the devil, and the Crown of Live is ours too, when we keep away from the temptations that the world has to offer.

In chapter five we look at three important keys to use as weapons to be set free from the devil's destructive exploits to ourselves, our loved ones, and those around us: 1) The forgiving heart and mind, 2) Intercessory prayer with the help of the Holy Spirit, and 3) Praise and Worship.

In chapter six, the Holy Spirit reminds us to be consciously aware of the need to be holy, as the Lord is holy. We learn from the book of Leviticus why the Lord commands us to be holy, and why we need to make a conscientious effort in setting ourselves apart from sinful living. When we live a life that is holy, pleasing, and acceptable to our Lord Jesus Christ, the Crown of Righteousness is ours.

Last, but not least, chapter seven is my encouragement to you to press on, be overcomers for Jesus Christ, and receive our everlasting reward, which is His Crown of Glory. We are now living in an ever-increasing violent and volatile world. But remember that it is the devil that is already defeated at the Cross! It is we who are living in victory because of what Jesus Christ has done on the Cross of Calvary! Hallelujah! AMEN!

Let's rejoice in the finished work of our Lord Jesus Christ, and let's march on victoriously to eternal glory, as we work together with our partner, the Holy Spirit to champion the salvation gospel of Jesus Christ, and to bring along as many people as we can into His Glorious Kingdom! The Crown of Rejoicing is ours when we see our loved ones and friends and strangers alike entering into His Glorious Kingdom along with us! Hallelujah! Amen and Amen!

1

Are you ready?

To all believers in Christ Jesus, how prepared are you to see His coming again? How prepared are you to stand before Him without fear of His judgment, see Him smiling at you, and rewarding you with His crown of Glory on your head, and hear Him say, **"Well done, thou good and faithful servant"**?

As I write, the Holy Spirit told me to tell you to start preparing now! It's not too late! So, how do we prepare for His coming? By getting ready to do battle with the forces of evil and darkness that has already begun to unleash their terror upon this earth like we have never seen before! Especially so in this 21st century because the devil knows that his time here on earth is getting shorter and shorter!

We do not know exactly when our Lord Jesus will return again. But we cannot afford to become complacent in our Christian walk, or find ourselves embroiled with worldly affairs and selfish ambitions until we lost sight of what Jesus told us to do in Matthew 24:42-44, **"Watch therefore, for you do not know what hour your Lord is coming…you also be ready, for the Son of Man is coming at an hour you do not expect."** We don't want to get caught unprepared, walking about in spiritual slumber when He comes suddenly, do we?

To the pre-believer equally loved by the Almighty Father, as you read this page, curious to know what this book is all about, God's Crown of

Glory can be yours, if you would just utter under your breath, in whatever circumstance or environment you are in right NOW, and ask Jesus Christ to come into your heart to be the Lord and Saviour of your life. Let me lead you in the sinner's prayer:

"Lord Jesus Christ, I acknowledge that I am a sinner, and that without You as my Lord and Saviour, I am lost in sin, trapped by addictions and by the world's devious ways. I acknowledge that Jesus Christ is the Son of God who died on the Cross for the salvation of man. His Blood shed for me has washed away all my sins, and reconciled me to God who is the Creator of heaven and earth. Thank You for Your salvation at the Cross. I invite you now to come into my heart and my life, to be my Lord and Saviour Jesus Christ! I am now forgiven, I am saved. I am loved by Jesus! I am Redeemed! Amen!"

CONGRATULATIONS! You are now a Child of God! Hallelujah! Praise the Lord! You are special in His eyes! You are a believer in Christ Jesus! So let's join in and get ready to do battle for His Kingdom to come! Amen!

Get ready, Warriors of God! March on boldly and fearlessly into His Glorious kingdom in the face of evil and destruction!

Before we begin, let's establish these truths:

"Devil, you are a LIAR, and you KNOW IT"!

"Devil, you are a COWARD, and you KNOW IT"!

"Devil, you are DEFEATED at the CROSS OF JESUS CHRIST and you KNOW IT!"

"As for me, I am FORGIVEN by JESUS CHRIST, washed by HIS BLOOD SHED ON THE CROSS FOR ME, and I KNOW IT!"

VICTORY is mine because CHRIST JESUS LIVES! HE IS RISEN! The bible declares it, and I declare it too! And I stand firmly on that TRUTH! AMEN!

Hallelujah! In Him there is NO CONDEMNATION!

"No matter how the devil tries his best to attack my past sins, they are ALL FORGIVEN AND NAILED TO THE CROSS of JESUS CHRIST"! Hallelujah!

"I am free"! "Jesus Christ is my REDEEMER"! "I am REDEEMED by His BLOOD"!

I DECLARE that I am the RIGHTEOUSNES of GOD in CHRIST JESUS, and I KNOW IT!

"Lord Jesus, I BELONG to YOU and YOU ALONE! I live only for YOU and YOU ALONE! My eyes are FOCUSED on YOU and Your RIGHTEOUSNESS, Your LOVELINESS, Your HOLINESS, Your PURITY, Your GOODNESS AND MERCY, so that I can emulate after you, and be transformed into Your likeness when You come to receive me into YOUR BEAUTIFUL, GLORIOUS, AND EVERLASTING KINGDOM! Amen!"

Hallelujah! Now that we have established these truths, let's look at the heavenly crowns which the apostles of Jesus talked about in the New Testament.

The Five Heavenly Crowns in the Bible

I. The Imperishable Crown – I Corinthians 9:24-25.

"Do you not know that those who run in a race all run, but one receives the prize? Run in such a way that you may obtain it. And everyone who competes for the prize is temperate in all things. Now they do it to obtain a perishable crown, but we for an imperishable crown."

Here, Paul urged the Corinthians to run the Christian life in such a way as to receive the reward at the end of that race. The Christian life, guided by the Holy Spirit, is one that is able to exercise self-control by crucifying every selfish desire in the flesh, and every ambition that seeks to glorify oneself. Along the way, the Christian points the way to others toward that beautiful, glorious eternal life through Jesus, and Jesus alone!

This crown is also described as the incorruptible inheritance by Peter in 1 Peter 1:3-4, reserved in heaven for believers who faithfully run the race without wavering in their faith and believe in Jesus Christ. All things on this earth are subject to decay and will perish. Jesus urged us not to store our treasures on earth "where moth and rust destroy, and where thieves break in and steal" (Matthew 6:19). The heavenly crown, however is "an inheritance incorruptible and undefiled and that does not fade away, reserved in heaven for you." The faithful Christian who endures the race to the end ultimately wins the heavenly reward.

II. The Crown of Rejoicing – 1 Thessalonians 2:19-20.

"For what is our hope, or joy, or crown of rejoicing? Is it not even you in the presence of our Lord Jesus Christ at His coming? For you are our glory and joy."

Paul's "crown of rejoicing" was his converts at the church in Thessalonica. They were his, together with Silvanus and Timothy, hope and joy when, on that glorious day, at the second coming of the Lord Jesus Christ, they and their converts will all enter into the Kingdom of Heaven together!

For Paul, there was no greater joy than seeing someone come to Christ. He considered his reward, known also as the soul winner's crown, as seeing the Thessalonians who received Christ as their personal Saviour meeting the Lord on that day of Rapture. Winning people to Christ is an eternal investment. It makes life worthwhile. What a day of rejoicing that will be! Those we win to Christ are our hope, joy and crown of glory!

The coming of Christ is a great motivation for us believers. We press on, albeit through many trials, persecution, chaos, uncertainty and tribulations. We keep sight of God's perspective on the purpose for our lives as Christians. When troubles come our way, we stay focus on Him as we look to Him as the author and finisher of our faith (Hebrews 12:2).

We rejoice greatly when we lead souls to Jesus! We are rewarded not only for the souls we win for Jesus. We are also rewarded for the influence we have on others, especially when we are able to praise Him with thankfulness in our hearts even in the midst of troubles and chaos all around us. We receive this crown when we are faithful in witnessing to the saving grace of Jesus with much gladness and rejoicing in our hearts. It is our greatest reward as we see souls coming to Jesus in great numbers! Hallelujah!

Luke tells us there is rejoicing even now in heaven (Luke 15:7). The crown of rejoicing will be our reward where "God will wipe away every tear . . . there shall be no more death, nor sorrow, nor crying. There shall be no more pain, for the former things have passed away" (Revelation 21:4). AMEN!

III. The Crown of Life – James 1:12 (Rev. 2:8-11).

"Blessed is the man who endures temptation; for when he has been approved, he will receive the crown of life which the Lord has promised to those who love Him."

In his letter to the Christian Jews, James sounded out his sense of urgency for them to live out their Christian life without doubt and double-mindedness in the face of trials, chaos, persecutions, and temptations which the world dangles before them.

James opened his letter by encouraging them to "count it all joy when you fall into various trials, knowing that the testing of your faith produces patience". He urged them to be steadfast in their faith in God "who gives to all liberally and without reproach" because of His grace for those who believe in Him. Therefore they must have resolute confidence in Him alone!

James also warned about the "filthiness and overflow of wickedness" which they must "lay aside". Only the "implanted Word" is "able to save your souls". From verses 19 to 27, he wrote earnestly about pursuing and upholding God's righteousness, holiness, and purity. This is the highest calling for all Christians to attain, especially so for Christians today, as we live in a world that's becoming extremely evil, wicked, and violent as we have never seen before!

In Matthew 5:11-12, Jesus warned us to be prepared for it: "Blessed are you when people insult you, persecute you and falsely say all kinds of evil against you because of me. Rejoice and be glad, because great is your reward in heaven."

IV. The crown of righteousness – 2 Timothy 4:8.

"Finally, there is laid up for me the crown of righteousness, which the Lord, the righteous Judge, will give to me on that Day, and not to me only but also to all who have loved His appearance."

Paul wrote this moving letter to Timothy towards the end of his ministry, as he was preparing himself for martyrdom in Jerusalem. In chapter 2, he encouraged young Timothy to "be strong in the grace that is in Christ Jesus…to "endure hardship as a good soldier of Jesus Christ" without becoming entangled "with the affairs of this life." Anyone who competes in any race is "not crowned unless he competes according to the rules". For Paul, he kept the rule by keeping the faith when he said in the preceding verse that "I have fought the good fight, I have finished the race, I have kept the faith."

This crown is assured to all those who are determined to pursue and uphold God's righteousness, holiness, and purity, with perseverance and longsuffering in the face of evil and wickedness, as they wait for that glorious day of His coming! It is the righteous Judge, Jesus Christ, who will judge according to our faith, and give us our crown which we deserve, having endured persecutions, sufferings, and even death.

V. The Crown of Glory – 1 Peter 5:1-4.

"The elders who are among you I exhort, I who am a fellow elder and a witness of the sufferings of Christ, and also a partaker of the glory that will be revealed;

Shepherd the flock of God which is among you, serving as overseers, not by compulsion but willingly, not for dishonest gain but eagerly;

Nor as being lords over those entrusted to you, but being examples to the flock;

And when the Chief Shepherd appears, you will receive the crown of glory that does not fade away."

Although Peter's address was to the elders spurring them to shepherd the flock of God, this crown of glory will also be rewarded to all those who fulfil their calling by sharing and spreading the gospel, no matter what their station in life is. The preaching and sharing of the good news need not be confined to full-time ministers only, as all Christians are called to share and spread the gospel of Jesus Christ.

This is the greatest achievement to fulfilling our calling, to run the race and finished the work God has called us to do here on earth. As Christians, we are also His children, and as His children, we become heirs of God and joint heirs with Christ, "if indeed we suffer with Him, that we may also be glorified" as Paul declared in Romans 8:17.

As we enter into His Kingdom, we are also entering into the likeness of Jesus Christ Himself. Paul eloquently expressed this in the following verse "For I consider that the sufferings of this present time are not worthy to be compared with the glory which shall be revealed in us." AMEN!

With these heavenly crowns in mind, let's march on to do battle with the forces of evil and wickedness!

3

Recognising the forces
we are battling with

Ephesians 6:12

> "For we do not wrestle against flesh and blood, but
> against principalities, against powers, against the
> rulers of the darkness of this age, against spiritual
> *hosts* of wickedness in the heavenly *places*"

3.1 Evil forces behind flesh

First, we need to understand that, for every attack, be it hurtful, abusive, malicious, or unkind words, or physical abuse, made against us by flesh, there is always some demonic influence controlling that flesh the devil is using to attack us. That flesh can be anyone. It can be your Pastor, your church leaders by whatever title they hold, or your fellow brothers and sisters in Christ. It can come from your family members, your close friends, your mentors, cult groups, terror groups, religious groups, or authorities who abuse their power. It can be anyone.

By now, you would already have had some people in mind, other than those I've already mentioned. Or they are the ones who are already attacking you right now! It can also be you attacking others! But they are NOT your enemies, and you are NOT their enemy. The DEVIL behind these attacks is the real ENEMY! You REBUKE the devil while you FORGIVE and PRAY for those who have hurt you, however bad it may be. You are not obliged to be friends with them forever, but forgive, let go, and move on. At the same time, you too have to learn to recognise the hurt you have done to others, repent and ask them to forgive you. If they refuse to forgive you, then ask the Lord to forgive you on their behalf. The act of forgiving, asking for forgiveness, and receiving forgiveness, is one of the major KEYS, and the first step, to winning battles against the devil!

The devil uses people to destroy each other. He also uses elements of this world to destroy mankind. But his weapons and activities can be limited for now, and ultimately eliminated altogether when Jesus comes again! Hallelujah! For as many as he can find to use and destroy, and elements he can use to turn into catastrophes, there are many more prayer warriors and intercessors that God can raise to pray and intercede against the devil and his wicked and destructive exploits. Intercessory prayer is another KEY to winning the battle against the devil, but we can pray and intercede only with the help of the Holy Spirit. Worship is another power KEY. We will look at these winning KEYS in the following chapters.

3.2 Evil forces destroying the image of God in man

Next, we need to recognise the parts in man which the devil goes all the way out to destroy. Man, as recorded in Genesis 1:26, is made in God's image:

> "Then God said, "Let Us make man in Our image, according
> to Our likeness; let them have dominion over the fish of the
> sea, over the birds of the air, and over the cattle, over all the
> earth and over every creeping thing that creeps on the earth."

In Leviticus 19:1-2, the Lord instructed Moses to tell the children of Israel to be like Him,

"Speak to all the congregation of the children
of Israel, and say to them: 'You shall be holy,
for I the LORD your God am holy.'"

In Proverbs 30 5-6, Agur the son of Jakeh declared:

"Every word of God is pure;
He is a shield to those who put their trust in Him.
Do not add to His words,
Lest He rebuke you,
And you be found a liar."

In Jeremiah 23:6, Jeremiah the prophet declared the Lord Jesus as:

"THE LORD OUR RIGHTEOUSNESS"

When Adam and Eve disobeyed God by eating from the fruit of the tree of knowledge of good and evil, which they were told not to eat, God's image and likeness in them broke immediately. Hence man's disobedience has given the devil the right to capitalise on that brokenness to destroy God's holiness, purity, and righteousness in man. The devil has also robbed man of his dominance over the whole earth, and had taken advantage of that dominance to destroy mankind, and everything that God has created altogether. Everything that God had created and saw them as good, the devil saw them as ugly and goes all the way out to destroy all that God had created.

So everyone of us walked about with different degrees of brokenness in our inner man vis-à-vis our family background, people in school, workplaces, organisations or institutions that we rubbed shoulders with, circumstances, mishaps or misfortunes that occurred beyond our control, lack of opportunities, being deprived of nurturing the innate gifts and talents in us, and other factors or deficits in our lives that would have had repercussions on our entire well-being. Our brokenness, left undetected, buried, and unresolved altogether, fester in us to becomes sore spots in our innermost being, which then gives the devil a foothold to use as weapons to destroy others, and sabotage ourselves. We need to know the truth about God's image in us, as it will help us to have the ability to recognise and command rejection to the devil's subtle whispers to our hearts and minds, for his destructive exploits.

3.3 Know the truth,
and the truth shall make you free – John 8:32

Let's look at the needful thing to do now. We need to be aware of the broken areas in our innermost being where the devil targets at and use them for his destructive exploits. We can be both his target for destruction as well as his weapon to destroy others. We really need to face up to this truth, because "My people are destroyed for lack of knowledge" (Hosea 4:6). In John 8:31-32, Jesus said to the Jews who believed in Him, "If you abide in My Word, you are My disciples indeed. And you shall know the truth, and the truth shall make you free."

All believers in Christ MUST know this truth Jesus describes about the devil and Himself in John 10:10, "The thief does not come except to steal and to kill, and to destroy. "I have come that they may have life, and that they may have it more abundantly." This is the truth about the devil that we Christians must be constantly on the lookout for, and the truth about Jesus that we must cling on to tenaciously if we want a life filled with blessings and abundance that come with a tag that say "His holiness, His purity, righteousness." God wants to bring out the best in us so that we can serve Him to the fullest and enjoy His blessings along the way. The devil does the total opposite by bringing out the worst in us so that he can use us to destroy others, and ultimately ourselves!

Unresolved broken areas in our lives become sore spots in our innermost being, which in turn, create a dangerous breeding ground in our inner man for the devil to capitalise on. If left raw for many years, and ultimately buried deep within us altogether, those sore spots will suddenly act up and wreak havoc through our reactions to some nonchalant or even frivolous remarks which inadvertently triggered them. Imagine, even the best of friends become bitter enemies immediately, each accusing the other of being "insensitive," of "exposing dirty linen," and the list goes on endlessly.

Our sore spots are areas in our innermost being that have been hurt and wounded through the years, along with the vicissitudes of our life. These then resulted in causing pain, shame and sorrow to our hearts, our emotions and our minds. When that storm or volcano erupted in us, even we ourselves are unable to control it. But if we are willing to confront and acknowledge those sore spots in us, however painful and/or shameful those sores are to us, surrender and yield them to Jesus for healing, restoration and wholeness, then we are taking the first important step to winning the battle against the devil. Remember, he is already defeated at the Cross of Jesus Christ. We don't have to be defeated by our pain and shame! We rise up as children of God, instead of being oppressed, suppressed, cowered and bullied by the devil!

What then, is the truth about our innermost being that the devil is working very hard for us to be ignorant of, so that he can steal, kill, and destroy us? The answer is found in Psalm 139:13-16:

"For You formed my inward parts;
You covered me in my mother's womb.
I will praise You, for I am fearfully and wonderfully made;
Marvellous are Your works,
And that my soul knows very well.
My frame was not hidden from You,
When I was made in secret,
And skilfully wrought in the lowest parts of the earth;
Your eyes saw my substance,
Being yet unformed.
And in Your book they all were written,
The days fashioned for me,
When as yet there were none of them."

Our innermost being is the sacred place where God's image resides. He made us with fear and wonder because He is a holy and delicate God. He imputed His image in us so that we can walk and have fellowship with Him in His likeness, clothed in the beauty of His Holiness, Purity, Righteousness, Glory, Grace, Loveliness, Tenderness, Loving-Kindness, and Wholeness. This is our artistic Abba Father, awesome in splendour, creating a physical body for Himself to delight in it!

The three most important parts He formed in us are our hearts, our souls, and our minds. They represent our entire holistic expressions toward Him as our Creator. He formed them as instruments in us to love Him and express our praise, worship and adoration toward Him with all our hearts, souls, and minds. That is why He commands us to love Him with all our hearts, with all our souls, and with all our minds in Matthew 22:37-38. We look at each part in the next chapter.

David understood and expressed the Lord's perfect revelation for our hearts, our souls, and our minds, in Psalm 19:7-10:

> "The law of the Lord is perfect, converting the soul;
> The testimony of the Lord is sure, making wise the simple;
> The statutes of the Lord are right, rejoicing the heart;
> The commandment of the Lord is pure, enlightening the eyes;
> The fear of the Lord is clean, enduring forever;
> The judgments of the Lord are true and righteous altogether.
> More to be desired are they than gold,
> Yea, than much fine gold;
> Sweeter also than honey and the honeycomb"

3.4 God's Redemptive plan for man

The Apostle Paul says in Acts 17:28 "for in Him we live and move and have our being."

Without God's wholesome image in us, our brokenness contributes to the obscuring of His highest calling for us to live as His children, to reflect His holiness, His purity, and His righteousness in us. But God has not left us in our broken state after the fall. Hallelujah! He has decreed a Redemptive plan for us through His Son Jesus Christ, as proclaimed in Luke 4:18-19

> "The Spirit of the Lord is upon Me,
> Because He has anointed Me to preach the gospel to the poor;
> He has sent Me to heal the broken-hearted;
> To proclaim liberty to the captives,
> And recovery of sight to the blind,
> To set at liberty those who are oppressed;
> To proclaim the acceptable year of the Lord"

Throughout the gospels, we read of how Jesus, being filled with the Holy Spirit, reached out with compassion to the lowly, the underdogs of society, those weighed down with illnesses and diseases, the demon-possessed, the broken-hearted, those who cry out for justice in a lopsided justice system, the curious, those looking for answers, and many more. In Luke's gospel we read of how Jesus healed and freed women who were suppressed and oppressed by society. In John 4:4-29 we read of the touching encounter between Jesus and the Samaritan woman. Jesus reached out to her when everyone else shunned her. After having had a brief conversation with Him, she turned from being a prostitute to becoming the first woman evangelist in the New Testament! Hallelujah!

Perhaps the best antidote Jesus had for them, and even more so for us today, as we are now living in an ever-increasing dark, violent, wicked world, can be found in His stirring Beatitude in Matthew 5:3-20:

> "Blessed are the poor in spirit,
> For theirs is the kingdom of heaven.
> Blessed are those who mourn,
> For they shall be comforted;

Blessed are the meek,

For they shall inherit the earth,

Blessed are those who hunger and thirst for righteousness,

For they shall be filled;

Blessed are the merciful,

For they shall obtain mercy;

Blessed are the pure in heart,

For they shall see God;

Blessed are the peacemakers,

For they shall be called sons of God;

Blessed are those who are persecuted for righteousness' sake,

For theirs is the kingdom of heaven."

The crown of Righteousness is ours when we have endured persecutions and sufferings for Jesus Christ and for the sake of the gospel. May I to invite you to read the Beatitude in your own quiet time, and ask the Holy Spirit to reveal personal insights to you, as you mediate on it. Refer to scholarly materials to help you understand the background to the Beatitude. May I also encourage you to read the four gospels so as to understand, and capture the heartbeat of the kingdom of heaven in your heart, and ask the Holy Spirit to guide you along. Stop to ponder, meditate, and ask questions, like how best can we, as God's children, live out His Kingdom here on earth, as we go about our daily life.

We sounded the alarm earlier on about how the devil targets the image of God in man by destroying the heart, soul, and mind of man. In the next chapter, we look at why the devil goes all out to destroy our hearts, souls, and minds.

4

Beware the devil!

1 Peter 5:8 "Be sober, be vigilant; because your adversary the devil walks about like a roaring lion, seeking whom he may devour."

Psalm 5:4-6 "For You are not a God who takes pleasure in wickedness; Nor shall evil dwell with You. The boastful shall not stand in Your sight; You hate all workers of iniquity. You shall destroy those who speak falsehood; The Lord abhors the bloodthirsty and deceitful man."

Psalm 51:6 "Behold, You desire truth in the innermost being; and in the hidden part You will make me know wisdom."

4.1 The vulnerable heart

Another word for 'devour' is to 'consume'. The devil targets at the three most important parts that God formed in man to steal, to kill, to destroy – the heart, the soul, the mind. Why? Because the first and great commandment given by Jesus in Matthew 22:37-38 says, "You shall love the Lord your God with <u>all</u> your <u>heart</u>, with <u>all</u> your <u>soul</u>, and with <u>all</u> your <u>mind</u>." The heart of man is the devil's main target to draw man away from God and to commit sins against Him. The devil's next target is the second commandment that follows in verse 39 that says <u>"You shall love your neighbour as yourself."</u> Paul warns the Galatians against "biting" and "devouring" one another, lest they fall into the danger of being "consumed by one another" (Galatians 5:15). The devil devours the heart and mind that is most vulnerable and unguarded by the <u>Word of God</u>.

So who are the vulnerable? Jesus said in Matthew 15:19

> "For out of the heart proceed evil thoughts, murders,
> adulteries, fornications, thefts, false witness, and blasphemies."

We read of the first account of murder in Genesis 4:5-8, where Cain murdered his brother Abel out of jealousy. Cain could not 'rule over' his rage as the Lord said he ought to. The Lord did not reject Cain altogether even though He rejected his offerings. He told Cain that his offerings would have been accepted if he had given the Lord a sacrificial offering.

Jeremiah the prophet tells us in chapter 17:9-10,

> "The heart is deceitful above all things,
> And desperately wicked; who can know it?
> "I, the Lord, search the heart, I test the mind,
> Even to give every man according to his ways,
> According to the fruit of his doings"

Hebrews 4:12-13 says,

> "For the Word of God is living and powerful, and sharper
> than any two-edged sword, piercing even to the division
> of soul and spirit, and of joints and marrow, and is a
> discerner of the thoughts and intents of the heart,
> "And there is no creature hidden from His sight, but all things are
> naked and open to the eyes of Him to whom we must give account."

Proverbs 4:23 tells us to "Keep your heart with all diligence, for out of it spring the issues of life."

The heart is the seat of man's state of mind. If we are not able to take ownership of the condition of our hearts, our thought processes will be affected and easily consumed by the "fiery darts of the wicked one" (Ephesians 6:16). We cannot always blame the devil when we slip into his trap and become his instrument to destroy others. All he did was to trigger the sore spots in our hearts and provoke our emotions. Then he sits back and watched us burst into violent reactions, unable to control the whirlwind that stirred in our hearts and reaches into our minds when we have become so bent in getting back at others.

Paul tells us in Ephesians 4:26-27, "Be angry, and do not sin: do not let the sun do down on your wrath, nor give place to the devil."

The apostle James warned us about blaming God as well when we are tempted to vengeful, malicious, or deceitful acts: "Let no one say when he is tempted, 'I am tempted by God'; for God cannot be tempted by evil, nor does He Himself tempt anyone. But each one is tempted when he is drawn away by his own desires and enticed. Then, when desire has conceived, it gives birth to sin; and sin, when it is full-grown, brings forth death" (James 1:13-15). He encourages us in chapter 4:7, "Therefore submit to God. Resist the devil and he will flee from you." The crown of live is ours when we are able to overcome temptation of sorts (James 1:12).

We guard ourselves from the "norms" of worldly wisdom and reactions to adversity by running to the bible to see what the living Word of Jesus has to say about our circumstances. We take encouragement from Jude in verses 20-21:

> "But you, beloved, building yourselves up on your
> most holy faith, praying in the Holy Spirit,
> Keep yourselves in the love of God, looking for the
> mercy of our Lord Jesus Christ unto eternal life.

4.2 The vulnerable mind

We need to take note here that the devil is good at quoting scriptures, and he does it better than any of us. He quotes scriptures to instil guilt and shame in us. He uses scriptures as weapons for Christians to slay one another. He is a fallen angel who has no right whatsoever, to quote or use scriptures to condemn God's children, even if he "presents" "the truth in love" about his targets. Remember, Christ has FORGIVEN US AT THE CROSS! In Him there is no condemnation! The use of scriptures as weapons to judge, condemn, suppress and oppress God's children is the act of manipulating, twisting, and desecrating of God's word by the devil. He is a sore loser, a coward, and a LIAR, going all out to provoke Christians to devour each other. The vulnerable mind of the high-and-mighty self-righteous, self-seeking Christian falls into this trap of using scriptures to justify the destructive intents of the vulnerable heart.

I have seen this happened too many times over. If an ordinary member in a church "sin" because he/she did not measure up to the "standard," or "expectation" of the church, or was stricken with sickness, or blew the whistle to something amiss, that member would get scripture verses thrown at him/her by "holier-than-thou," self-righteous leaders and members alike. Worst still, they "pray" and make that person "read" bible verses to "help you see where you might have gone wrong!" Or they become cold toward that person, gave him/her the silent treatment, and gang up to ostracise or marginalise that person, thus making it unbearable enough for him/her to leave the church to prevent the attack from escalating further! The vulnerable and depraved mind has no idea what it means to "love your neighbour as yourself."

Then again, the devil also uses scriptures to help find an "excuse" when someone sins. The devil has one favourite scripture which he dishes out especially for a particular group of people. He loves to quote from Jesus in Matthew 26:41. But the devil deliberately omits the first part and quotes only the second part which says "The spirit is indeed willing, but the flesh is weak." Paul warned the Corinthians in 2 Corinthians 11:14 that "Satan himself transforms himself into an angel of light."

The vulnerable mind latches onto this second part immediately and uses it to justify the actions of the vulnerable heart. Neglect in reading the bible, or reading without understanding, neglect in meditating on scriptures, and in spending quiet time with God, has deprived the mind of its ability to point out to the devil, that the damaging actions could have been prevented if the mind had given thought to the warning of Jesus in the first part, which says, "Watch and pray, lest you enter into temptation."

In this instance, while the ordinary church member would be slayed with scriptures without hesitation, a different tune was sung altogether for an "aristocrat," or a businessman of high social standing. This particular person suddenly appeared in the news, surprising everyone. He had been summoned to court for misappropriating some funds, or was filed for divorce by his wife because his "second family" suddenly appeared out of nowhere, or for whatever reasons that warranted public attention. Nobody knew about his furtive life until the law brought it to light. Yet those very same "holier-than-thou" self-righteous leaders and those wanting to be seen in public as "highly spiritual," rallied around that person during a press conference to pronounce him "forgiven," by the church, because "Jesus says so," and because "the spirit is indeed willing, but the flesh is weak." "To err is human," they added with an air of religiosity about them.

The devil has won in this arena, because the vulnerable mind has yet to crucify the bias mind-set of the world to the Cross of Jesus Christ. Paul says in Romans 8:5-7,

"For those who live according to the flesh set their minds on the things of the flesh, but those who live according to the Spirit, the things of the Spirit.

> For to be carnally minded is death, but to be
> spiritually minded is life and peace;
> Because the carnal mind is enmity against God; for it is
> not subject to the law of God, nor indeed can be.
> So then, those who are in the flesh cannot please God."

Paul told the Christians in Galatians 2:6,

> "But from those who seemed to be something –
> whatever they were, it makes no difference to me; God
> shows personal favouritism to no man – for those who
> seemed to be something added nothing to me."

We need to crucify the bias mind-set of the world and put on the mind-set of Christ instead. Paul beseeched us in Romans 12:2-3,

> "And do not be conformed to this world, but be
> transformed by the renewing of your mind, that you
> may prove what is that good and acceptable and perfect
> will of God. For I say, through the grace given to me,
> to everyone who is among you, not to think of himself
> more highly than he ought to think, but to think soberly,
> as God has dealt to each one a measure of faith."

Paul tells us how to treat each other in verses 9 & 10:

> "Let love be without hypocrisy. Abhor what is evil. Cling
> to what is good. Be kindly affectionate to one another with
> brotherly love, in honour giving preference to one another."

James 3:13-18 gives a clear comparison between earthly wisdom and wisdom from above:

> "Who is wise and understanding among you?
> Let him show by good conduct that his works
> are done in the meekness of wisdom.
> But if you have bitter envy and self-seeking in your
> hearts, do not boast and lie against the truth.
> This wisdom does not descend from above,
> but is earthly, sensual, demonic.

> For where envy and self-seeking exist,
> confusion and every evil thing are there.
> But the wisdom that is from above is first pure, then
> peaceable, gentle, willing to yield, full of mercy and good
> fruits, without partiality and without hypocrisy."

When Paul spoke about "speaking the truth in love" in Ephesians chapter 4, he was referring to the diversity of gifts that God gave to some in church "for the equipping of the saints for the work of ministry, for the edifying of the body of Christ" (verse 12), "till we all come to the unity of the faith and of the knowledge of the Son of God" (verse 13). God's purpose for church ministry is to edify, or build, each other in the knowledge of the love, grace, and mercy of Jesus Christ. Jesus did not come to tear us apart, but to bring us into His saving grace. Who are we then to use that knowledge to devour, and tear each other down?

Paul further urged the saints in Ephesus to grow into maturity, instead of being easily swayed by "Every wind of doctrine, by the trickery of men, in the cunning craftiness of deceitful plotting, but speaking the truth in love, may grow up in all things into Him who is the head – Christ – from whom the whole body, joined and knit together by what every joint supplies, according to the effective working by which every part does its share, causes growth of the body for the edifying of itself in love" (verses 14-16).

Let's heed the advice of Peter in 1 Peter 1:13-16,

> "Therefore gird up the loins of your mind, be sober, and rest
> your hope fully upon the grace that is to be brought to you
> at the revelation of Jesus Christ; as obedient children, not
> conforming yourselves to the former lusts, as in your ignorance;
> but as He who called you is holy, you also be holy in all your
> conduct, because it is written, 'Be holy, for I am holy.'

4.3 The vulnerable soul

Then, if the devil finds it hard to devour our hearts and minds, he goes after our soul, the part in us which the devil works on relentlessly to lure our five senses – sight, sound, touch, smell and taste – to the trappings of the world. He dangles before us all that are enticing and desirable to our senses.

John urged his disciples not to be drawn by the world in 1 John 2:15-17,

> "Do not love the world or the things in the world.
> If anyone loves the world, the love of the Father is not in him.
> For all that is in the world – the lust of the flesh, the lust of the eyes,
> and the pride of life – is not of the Father but is of the world.
> And the world is passing away, and the lust of it; but
> he who does the will of God abides forever."

Paul urged young Timothy in 2 Timothy 2:22 to:

> "Flee also youthful lusts; but pursue righteousness,
> faith, love and peace, along with those who
> call on the Lord out of a pure heart."

Paul has this to say to the Thessalonians in 1 Thessalonians 4:3-5,

> "For this is the will of God, your sanctification: that
> you should abstain from sexual immorality; that
> each of you should know how to possess his own
> vessel in sanctification and honour, not in passion of
> lust, like the Gentiles who do not know God."

Paul has strong words against those who knowingly "suppress" the truth of God's attributes and image with ungodly, unclean and unrighteous living. In his letter to the Romans, he stated strongly that the ungodly, blinded by foolish wisdom and darkened minds, will ultimately pay for the consequence of their mockery towards God.

We need to take heed of Paul's warning in Romans 1:24-32 in absolute terms,

"Therefore God also gave them up to uncleanness, in the lust
of their hearts, to dishonour their bodies among themselves,
"who exchanged the truth of God for the lie, and worshipped and served
the creature rather than the Creator, who is blessed forever. Amen.
"For this reason God gave them up to vile passions. For even their
women exchanged the natural use for what is against nature.
"Likewise also the men, leaving the natural use of the woman, burned in
their lust for one another, men with men committing what is shameful,
and receiving in themselves the penalty of their error which was due.
"And even as they did not like to retain God in their
knowledge, God gave them over to a debased mind,
to do those things which are not fitting;
"being filled with all unrighteousness, sexual immorality,
wickedness, covetousness, maliciousness; full of envy, murder,
strife, deceit, evil-mindedness; they are whisperers,
"backbiters, haters of God, violent, proud, boasters,
inventors of evil things, disobedient to parents,
"undiscerning, untrustworthy, unloving, unforgiving, unmerciful;
"who, knowing the righteous judgment of God, that those
who practice such things are deserving of death, not only do
the same but also approve of those who practice them."

God's Holiness, Purity and Righteousness cannot be compromised whatsoever!

"I AM WHO I AM"

as He declares in Exodus 3:14, lovingly "created man in His own image; in the image of God He created him; male and female He created them" (Genesis 1:27) to share His Holiness, Purity, Righteousness, His Glory, His Loveliness, His Beauty, His Splendour, His tenderness, His loving-kindness,

His goodness, His mercies, with them. He created them because He delights Himself in them, and He expects them to reciprocate that love to Him. In verse 28, He blessed them and told them to "Be fruitful and multiply."

Yet man chose to rebel against Him without even blinking an eye! God made male to demonstrate His masculinity, and female to demonstrate His tenderness, to put it simply. He puts them together to complement each other, to enjoy and share their lives together as man and woman and to procreate. God saw that it was good. The jealous devil saw it as evil.

God has suffered, and is still suffering much ridicule, rejection and mockery. Yet He is still waiting patiently, with much love and longsuffering, for those who would turn to Him and repent of their sins. He is ever ready to forgive simply because He is LOVE. Can you sense the heartbeat of Him whose holy, pure and righteous intentions have been desecrated?

God created our body to be the temple of the Holy Spirit. When Paul urged the Christians in 1 Corinthians 6:19-20 to flee from sexual immorality, he asked them this question:

> "Or do you not know that your body is the temple
> of the Holy Spirit who is in you, whom you have
> from God, and you are not your own?"
> For you were bought at a price; therefore glorify God in
> your body and in your spirit, which are God's."

Peter begged the pilgrims and sojourners of the Dispersion in 1 Peter 2:11 to "abstain from fleshly lusts which war against the soul." The unbelieving stumbles about in the darkness of the sins of this world, but believers in Christ walk in the light of God's Word. Peter says in verses 9-10 of the same chapter,

> "But you are a chosen generation, a royal priesthood,
> a holy nation, His own special people, that you
> may proclaim the praises of Him who called you
> out of darkness into His marvellous light;

Who once were not a people but are now the people of God,
who had not obtained mercy but now have obtained mercy."

Let's not get drawn or enticed by the sinful ways of this world. Let's be encouraged by what Hebrews 12:1-2 have to say about running the race of faith,

"Therefore we also, since we are surrounded by so great
a cloud of witnesses, let us lay aside every weight, and
the sin which so easily ensnares us, and let us run with
endurance the race that is set before us, - verse 1
Looking unto Jesus, the author and finisher of our faith, who for the
joy that was set before Him endured the cross, despising the shame,
and has sat down at the right hand of the throne of God." – verse 2

The imperishable crown is ours when we honour the Lord with our bodies. Let's make a conscientious effort in fixing our eyes on Jesus at all times, looking neither to the right nor to the left. Please join me in singing this beautiful song, "Turn your eyes upon Jesus."

4.4 Seven things the Lord hates

We need to know what the Word of God has to say about the sins of this world. We must keep watch at all times and be alert enough to stop the devil in his track, and resist him each time he tries to creep into our hearts, our souls and our minds. In Proverbs 6:16-19, the Lord clearly states what He hates:

"These six things the Lord hates. Yes, seven are an abomination to Him:

- ➢ A proud look
- ➢ A lying tongue
- ➢ Hands that shed innocent blood
- ➢ A heart that devises wicked plans
- ➢ Feet that are swift in running to evil
- ➢ A false witness who speaks lies
- ➢ And one who sows discord among brethren.

With Proverbs 6:16-19 in mind, the next thing we need to do, is to heed the advice of Paul in Ephesians 5:15-16, "See then that you walk circumspectly, not as fools but as wise, redeeming the time, because the days are evil."

4.5 The blessed man verses the ungodly man

How then do we walk circumspectly? Psalms Chapter One provides the answer. It gives a beautiful analogy between the Righteous and the ungodly.

"Blessed is the man,
Who walks not in the counsel of the ungodly,
Nor stands in the path of sinners,
Nor sits in the seat of the scornful;
But his delight is in the law of the Lord,
And in His law he meditates day and night.
He shall be like a tree,
Planted by the rivers of water,
That brings forth its fruit in its season,
Whose leaf also shall not wither;
And whatever he does shall prosper.
The ungodly are not so,
But are like the chaff which the wind drives away.
Therefore the ungodly shall not stand in the judgment,
Nor sinners in the congregation of the righteous
For the Lord knows the way of the righteous,
But the way of the ungodly shall perish."

The crown of Righteousness belongs to the blessed man. He is 'set apart' from the world to live as God's sanctified people, washed by the blood of Jesus Christ at the Cross of Calvary. A people called to consecrate themselves to live a life that reflects God's Holiness, Purity, and Righteousness. This is the prayer of Jesus to His Father in John 17:15-19,

"I do not pray that You should take them out of the
world, but that You should keep them from the evil one"
"They are not of the world, just as I am not of the world"
"Sanctify them by Your truth. Your Word is truth"
"As You sent Me into the world, I also have sent them into the world"
"And for their sakes I sanctify Myself, that they
also may be sanctified by the truth."

In a nutshell, Jesus prayed to His Father to keep His followers from evil, from being corrupted by the world, and from the power and craftiness of Satan, by sanctifying them with the truth of His Father's Word.

Peter encouraged the pilgrims of the Dispersion in I Peter 3:15 to:

"Sanctify the Lord God in your hearts, and always be
ready to give a defense to everyone who asks you a reason
for the hope that is in you, with meekness and fear."

Sanctification is a process which we need to subject our flesh to each day, even though our spirit man is saved through the washing of the blood of Jesus Christ at the Cross. We need the Word of God and the revelation of the Holy Spirit to help us with this process, as our flesh is still weak. Only God knows the true intents and thoughts of our hearts and minds more than we do. David was acutely aware of this when he expressed it in Psalm 139:23-34,

"Search me, O God, and know my heart;
Try me, and know my anxieties;
And see if there is any wicked way in me,
And lead me in the way everlasting."

Paul says that, since we are sanctified by the blood of Jesus, we offer ourselves as living sacrifices, holy and acceptable in our thoughts, words, and deeds toward Him, and toward one another. He encourages us in Hebrews 10:19-25,

"Therefore, brethren, having boldness to
enter the Holiest by the blood of Jesus,
By a new and living way which He consecrated for
us, through the veil, that is, His flesh,
And having a High Priest over the house of God,
Let us draw near with a true heart in full assurance of
faith, having our hearts sprinkled from an evil conscience
and our bodies washed with pure water.
Let us hold fast the confession of our hope without
wavering, for He who promised is faithful.
And let us consider one another in order to stir up love and good works,
Not forsaking the assembling of ourselves together, as is
the manner of some, but exhorting one another, and so
much the more as you see the Day approaching."

5

Weapons for spiritual battle

In chapter three, we talked about the need to recognise who we are wrestling with. Paul tells us in Ephesians 6:10-18 that our warfare is against principalities, powers, rulers of the darkness of this age, and against spiritual hosts of wickedness in the heavenly places.

5.1 Put on the whole armour of God

We look at the weapons which Paul tells us to equip ourselves with in order to do spiritual battle:

"Finally, my brethren, be strong in the Lord
and in the power of His might.
Put on the whole armour of God that you may be
able to stand against the wiles of the devil.
For we do not wrestle against flesh and blood, but against
principalities, against powers, against the rulers of the darkness of
this age, against spiritual hosts of wickedness in the heavenly places
Therefore take up the whole armour of God that you may be able
to withstand in the evil day, and having done all, to stand.
Stand therefore, having girded your waist with truth,
having put on the breastplate of righteousness,
"And having shod your feet with the preparation of the gospel of peace;

> Above all, taking the shield of faith with which you will be
> able to quench all the fiery darts of the wicked one.
> And take the helmet of salvation, and the sword
> of the Spirit, which is the Word of God;
> Praying always with all prayer and supplication
> in the Spirit, being watchful to this end with all
> perseverance and supplication for all the saints"

As Paul reasoned in 2 Corinthians 10:3-5, "For though we walk in the flesh, we do not war according to the flesh. For the weapons of our warfare are not carnal but mighty in God for pulling down strongholds, casting down arguments and every high thing that exalts itself against the knowledge of God, bringing every thought into captivity to the obedience of Christ."

We identified three **KEYS** to winning spiritual battles against the devil and his spiritual hosts of wickedness.

5.2 Key #1 - The forgiving heart and mind

Forgiveness is the first crucial weapon to pulling down strongholds. Why? Because an unforgiving heart is the devil's greatest weapon to challenge and attack the new covenant made by Jesus in Matthew 26:28, "For this is My blood of the new covenant, which is shed for many for the remission of sins." The Lord's Supper is one of the most touching moments between Jesus and His disciples before His crucifixion. For our sins to be remitted, or forgiven, and our transgressions pardoned, Jesus had to shed His precious blood to redeem us from our sins.

It was for this very reason that Jesus taught us to pray in Matthew 6:9-13,

> "In this manner, therefore, pray:
> "Our Father in heaven, Hallowed be Your name,
> "Your kingdom come. Your will be done
> On earth as it is in heaven.
> "Give us this day our daily bread.

"And forgive us our debts,
As we forgive our debtors.
"And do not lead us into temptation,
But deliver us from the evil one.
For Yours is the kingdom
And the power and the glory forever
Amen.

Jesus further singled out the need to forgive in verses 14 and 15, **"For if you forgive men their trespasses, your heavenly Father will also forgive you. But if you do not forgive men their trespasses, neither will your Father forgive your trespasses."** Just as He was about to give His life freely for the forgiveness of our sins, Jesus revealed the essence of His heart to the Jews when He told them of the need to forgive others. He knew that the Jews would take to heart those that had done them wrong, and would not let any issues or injuries pass until revenge had been exacted. How then, can they expect their heavenly Father to forgive them of their trespasses against Him, if they refuse to forgive others who trespassed against them? So instead of becoming vindictive, Jesus encouraged the Jews to forgive those who trespassed against them.

His teaching on forgiving one's enemy contradicted that of the Jewish rabbis' traditional teachings. In the preceding chapter in Matthew 5:43-45, Jesus said to them:

"You have heard that it was said, 'You shall love your neighbour
and hate your enemy.' "But I say to you, love your enemies,
bless those who curse you, do good to those who hate you,
and pray for those who spitefully use you and persecute you,
"That you may be sons of your Father in heaven; for
He makes His sun rise on the evil and on the good,
and sends rain on the just and on the unjust"

Jesus was bringing home the point that, by loving our enemies, blessing, praying and forgiving those who device ill-intentions towards us, we are demonstrating to others what it means to become sons of God. When Jesus died in our place, He redeemed us from becoming spiritual orphans to being reconciled to His Father in heaven. We cannot enter into a spiritual relationship with His Father if we are not forgiven of our sins. Neither can we enjoy that special relationship as His sons if we refuse to forgive others even as He has forgiven us unconditionally. That was why Jesus told Peter in Matthew 18:22 to forgive "up to seventy times seven."

If we do not guard our hearts with this truth, to forgive as Jesus Christ has forgiven us, the devil will gleefully capitalise on our unforgiving hearts to thwart our special relationship with our Father in heaven. To whatever extent that we have been provoked, we must guard against letting the devil get the better of us. Paul encouraged the Christians at Corinth to forgive the offender in their church "lest Satan should take advantage of us; for we are not ignorant of his devices" (2 Corinthians 2:11). As Paul had determined in his heart to forgive the offender, he urged the Corinthians to do likewise, and exhorted them to restore the offender back into their fellowship with love and comfort.

Paul warned about not forgiving and comforting the offender, for fear that the offender might be "swallowed up with too much sorrow" (2 Corinthians 2:7). Unforgiving on the part of the Corinthians, and sorrow on the part of the offender, will leave room in their hearts for the devil to plant his strongholds, which would ultimately lead to strings of bitter quarrels and divisions in the church. This will further lead to the falling out of the purpose of the church, that is, to come together as sons of our Father in heaven to offer Him our praises and worship, thanksgiving, adoration, and fellowship in His love with one another.

If we cannot have agape love for one another, and we are always occupied over petty issues, or over some individuals, we will not be able to enter into that special relationship with our Father in heaven. No matter how hard we try, with singing and praying, and going through one liturgy after another, the devil will see to it that our hearts and minds are so consumed with those things that we get distracted from having true fellowship with our Father, and with one another.

We cannot, and must not, let the devil turn the church, which Jesus birthed forth at the Cross, into his playground for his destructive exploits! We need to take heed of what Jesus said in Matthew 15:19 "For out of the heart proceed evil thoughts, murders, adulteries, fornications, thefts, false witness, blasphemies." These, and those spelt out in Proverbs 6:16-19 and Romans 1:24-32, are the devil's strongholds which we need to be mindful of. We pull down these strongholds with the whole armour of God, which is found in His Word.

Paul encouraged the Christians in Ephesus with these words, "Let not corrupt word proceed out of your mouth, but what is good for necessary edification, that it may impart grace to the hearers. And do not grieve the Holy Spirit of God, by whom you were sealed for the day of redemption. Let all bitterness, wrath, anger, clamour, and evil speaking be put away from you, with all malice. And be kind to one another, tender-hearted, forgiving one another, even as God in Christ forgave you." (Verse 29-32).

Paul's encouragement to the Christians in Philippi best sum up how we Christians ought to treat each other in Philippians 4:8-9,

> "Finally, brethren, whatever things are true, whatever
> things are noble, whatever things are just, whatever things
> are pure, whatever things are lovely, whatever things
> are of good report, if there is any virtue and if there is
> anything praiseworthy – meditate on these things.
> The things which you learned and received and heard, and saw
> in me, these do, and the God of peace will be with you."

5.3 Key #2 - Intercessory prayer with the help of the Holy Spirit

The next key weapon for spiritual battle is that of **intercessory prayer**. As sons of our Father in heaven, we are given the authority to defeat demons and pray for the sick with the help of the Holy Spirit. We need the Holy Spirit because the battle does not belong to us but to God. This was God's assurance to King Jehoshaphat when he cried out to the Lord because he was threatened by a "great multitude" coming against his kingdom. We read in 2 Chronicles 20:15 that God spoke through Jahaziel to Judah:

> "Listen, all you of Judah and you inhabitants of Jerusalem,
> and you King Jehoshaphat; Thus says the LORD to you:
> 'Do not be afraid nor dismayed because of this great
> multitude, for the battle is not yours, but God's.'"

Just before Jesus was taken up in a cloud to be seated with His Father in heaven, He told his disciples in Acts 1:8

> "But you shall receive power when the Holy Spirit has come
> upon you; and you shall be witnesses to Me in Jerusalem,
> and in all Judea and Samaria, and to the end of the earth."

We read throughout the book of Acts of the signs and wonders, healings and deliverance that followed those who were filled with the Holy Spirit and spoke with other tongues.

In Mark 16:17-18, after Jesus had risen from His finished work on the Cross, He gave this mandate to His disciples:

> "And these signs will follow those who believe: In My name
> they will cast out demons, they will speak with new tongues;
> "They will take up serpents; and if they drink anything
> deadly, it will by no means hurt them; they will lay
> hands on the sick, and they will recover."

Jesus said to His disciples in Luke 10:18-19:

> "I saw Satan fall like lightning from heaven.
> "Behold, I give you the authority to trample on serpents
> and scorpions, and over all the power of the enemy,
> and nothing shall by any means hurt you."

HALLELUJAH! Amen! Satan is defeated! Let's rejoice in the Lord for His goodness, His grace, and His mercies!

In John 14:15-17, Jesus says to His disciples:

> "If you love me, keep My commandments
> "And I will pray the Father, and He will give you another
> Helper, that He may abide with you forever
> "the Spirit of truth, whom the world cannot receive,
> because it neither sees Him nor knows Him; but you know
> Him, for He dwells with you and will be in you."

We need the Holy Spirit to help us pray and intercede in the spirit realm. Paul understood the need for believers in Jesus Christ to be filled with the Holy Spirit, so that the Holy Spirit might help us walk according to the Spirit of God, instead of the flesh. He argued in this vein to the Christians in Rome about the role of the Holy Spirit in the life of "those who are in Christ." While he acknowledged that the flesh is still weak, Christians have no excuse to continue to be carnal minded because we have been adopted as sons of our Father whom we have the privilege to call "Abba Father." Jesus called His Father "Abba" in Mark 14:36, as an expression of deep love and fellowship with His Father.

As adopted sons of our Abba Father, we are also heirs through Christ His Son, who has redeemed us from the bondages of the sinful elements of this world. We are therefore no longer slaves to the world. We can cry out "Abba Father" when we are overwhelmed by the sins of this world because we are given the privileged to do so, as Paul says in Galatians 4:6,

"And because you are sons, God has sent forth the Spirit
of His Son into your hearts, crying out, "Abba Father!"

In view of our weaknesses, Paul said that if the Spirit of God dwells in us,
He will bear witness with our spirit that, as sons of God, we are no longer
subject to the bondage of the flesh. We are instead led by the Spirit of God
to be spiritually minded, which is "life and peace" (Romans 8:6). Paul went
on to say in verses 26-27,

"Likewise the Spirit also helps in our weaknesses. For we
do not know what we should pray for as we ought, but the
Spirit Himself makes intercession for us with groanings
which cannot be uttered. Now He who searches the hearts
knows what the mind of the Spirit is, because He makes
intercession for the saints according to the will of God."

The will of God in the spirit realm is for all His saints to walk on this
earth free from the clutches of the devil and his strongmen. We are to walk
according to the Glory of the New Covenant which Jesus Christ has given
to us in His commandments. In 2 Corinthians 3:17-18, Paul says

"Now the Lord is the Spirit; and where the
Spirit of the Lord is, there is liberty.
But we all, with unveiled face, beholding as in a mirror the
glory of the Lord, are being transformed into the same image
from glory to glory, just as by the Spirit of the Lord."

I remember, during one of my quite time worshipping and praying in
tongues, the Holy Spirit suddenly showed me broken areas in my innermost
being that needed healing. I was stunned for a moment. I then asked Him
how to go about doing it, as I was at a total loss in the area of inner healing.
It was also something that I have not heard of. At that time, I was overseas,
and had just completed my studies. My plan was to stay on and look for
a part-time job, before continuing on with my post-graduate studies the
following year.

I was stunned again when the Holy Spirit told me to go home, fly back to my own country. So I asked Him some questions. What should I do, even if I go back home? Can healing not be done here instead of back home? I was reluctant to go back as I had looked forward to another year of study. He replied by asking me which was more important, to continue living in a state of brokenness, and not knowing why the same things were always happening to me, or to be healed and be set free from generational curses? I struggled with this, and other issues that gripped my life, which the Holy Spirit revealed to me, for the next few days.

When I finally agreed to return home, the Holy Spirit instructed me to contact an old time friend immediately after flying home. I got in touch with this friend of mind the day after I arrived home. I shared with him what the Holy Spirit had revealed to me. I did not hear from him again until about a month later. He called me over the phone and told me to contact a certain person who had a deep inner healing ministry. I contacted this person immediately, and my journey to healing, wholeness, and freedom from generational curses began the following year.

Four years later, the Lord opened the door for me to go back to that same country to pursue my post-graduate studies. This time round, I was ready to fly back home again after completing my studies, when the Holy Spirit told me to do so. He wasted no time in revealing to me personally, the need for me to break demonic strongholds that had a hold over my life because of my family lineage's deep involvement with blood ties, and ancestral and idol worship. Now, being aware of my spiritual state, and having learnt about the principalities and powers of darkness and spiritual hosts of wickedness and destructive exploits, I was ready for the next level of spiritual warfare.

Since this was another spiritual dimension which involves warfare, the Holy Spirit instructed me to tune in to Pastor Benny Hinn's teachings on Spiritual warfare and demonology. I spent two whole days in front of my laptop listening to his teachings on YouTube and typing out every word and every sentence he said. When he came to the part where he identified the twelve strongmen, each with its own destructive exploits, the Holy Spirit quickened to me the strongmen that had been tormenting me all those years. He told me to get ready to cast them out of my life after the two days of intense listening.

With my New King James Bible in one hand opened to Luke 10:18-20, I began by reading those verses out loud. I then called out the first strongman to listen to the scripture, as I read it again. Remember, demons are COWARDS! When they begin to realise that you know your position and standing in the resurrected Christ, and that you are able to handle the Word of God appropriately, they will try to buy time to stay because they know they will ultimately have to flee in the presence of the Holy Spirit who is in you! They will try to stall their eviction by making you remember your "sins." Remember also that they are liars! I told him that the blood of Jesus Christ shed on the Cross of Calvary has washed away ALL my "sins", and they are remembered NO MORE because I am FORGIVEN OF MY SINS!

When I sensed that the strongman began to shake at the mention of the blood of Jesus Christ, I immediately turned to Matthew 26:28, and read it aloud to the strongman. I turned back to Luke 10:18-20, and said to this coward, "All authority have been given to me by Jesus Christ, whose authority have been given to Him by His Father in heaven. As heirs and joint heirs with Jesus Christ, the Son of God, I, as the child of my Father in heaven, take this same authority given to me as His child, and COMMAND you to leave right now! You have no more place in here, as this body belongs to the temple of the Holy Spirit, and the Holy Spirit ALONE! You might as well leave now. Otherwise I will keep tormenting and bombarding you with scriptures! The coward left immediately! Hallelujah! There's power in the blood of Jesus Christ! Sing it with me!

I called out the next coward which the Holy Spirit identified for me. I applied the same strategy to this coward, and he left immediately! The Holy Spirit told me to rest for the day, and I thanked the Lord with this prayer: "Father in heaven, thank you for setting me free from the two demonic strongholds. I seal this work today with the blood of Jesus Christ, and I asked for the blood of Jesus to build a hedge around and above me, to protect me from any vengeance from the demons. Thank you once again, for your love for me. I pray in Jesus' name. Amen."

For the next three days, a total of four cowards were evicted from me, one after another, spread over those days. The Holy Spirit then told me to move on to praising and worshipping the Triune God. Other unclean spirits of lesser power and strength, which had tagged along with those strongmen, will flee when the name of God the Father, Jesus the Son, and the Holy Spirit, is glorified and exalted through our praises and worship! We focus on singing and worshipping the Triune God with all our hearts, our souls, and our minds. This is most effective in warding off any demonic distractions that might hinder us from our fellowship with our Abba Father.

5.4 Key # 3 - Praise and Worship

Praise and Worship are the most powerful weapons for Christians. We ought to engage in it at all times, both in good times and in bad times. We ought to have only one hobby in our spirit, that of singing praises and worship in our hearts to the Triune God always, at all times! The bible records songs of prayer in times of need and protection, praises in times of thanksgiving, and worship for all occasions.

When we worship and praise the Lord with all our hearts, our souls, and our minds, we are inviting Him to dwell in our hearts. As David says in Psalm 22:3-5,

> "But You are holy,
> Enthroned in the praises of Israel.
> Our fathers trusted in You;
> They trusted, and You delivered them.
> They cried to You, and were delivered;
> They trusted in You, and were not ashamed."

Mighty things happen when we worship with hands lifted up to the Triune God. We read in Exodus 14, of how the Lord divided the Red sea for the children of Israel to cross over, when Moses lifted up his rod and stretched out his hand over the sea in obedience to the Lord. We saw what happened in Acts 16, when Paul and Silas were praying and singing hymns to God while they were in prison. Chains were loosed, and doors were opened.

We can be set free from our spiritual chains and bondages when we obey the Lord by giving Him our praises and worship with awe and reverence. Blessings will come our way when we praise and worship Him without ceasing. Even when ugly things happen in our lives, we still praise Him. That was what the Lord challenged me, some years back, when I pondered over those things that had happened while I was studying in a Bible College. As I waited upon Him one early morning, He whispered in my heart with this question, "Would you still be able to praise me, despite all that had happened?" I paused for a moment. When I said "Yes", He put a song in my heart. I would like to share it with you.

He deserves our praises
In good times and bad times
He deserves our praises
When all has been said and done
He deserves our praises
Even though life seems to be at odds
He deserves our praises
Because He is the Sovereign Lord

He deserves our praises
In the midst of life's storms
He deserves our praises
Because He keeps us going on
He deserves our praises
Even when our hopes and dreams fade away

He deserves our praises
Because He will lead the way

So let's just praise Him
And call upon His name
The name of Jesus
Who will always be the same
He is standing and waiting
For all those who will run to Him
So let's just praise Him
And call upon His name.
(This entire song is author's own composition)

Coming back to where the Holy Spirit told me to set aside time for praise and worship, He again instructed me to tune in to Pastor Benny Hinn's various worship services, posted on YouTube. As I began to follow the worship services every morning, closing my eyes and lifting up my hands to the Lord, worshipping Him for almost the whole morning, lost in His love and presence, intoxicated by those love songs, with tears running down my cheeks, slowly but surely, unclean spirits started coming out, one after another.

Each day as I worship and praise Him, I ask the Holy Spirit to search my heart and mind. As I read the bible, I ask Him to sanctify my innermost being with the Word of God, and help me purge out any unclean spirits that may still lurk within me. I bless Abba Father, and thank Him for His love, grace and mercy shown to me. Psalm 103:1-5 is one of my favourites:

"Bless the Lord, O my soul;
And all that is within me, bless His holy name!
Bless the Lord, O my soul;
And forget not all His benefits:
Who forgives all your iniquities,
Who heals all your diseases,

Who redeems your life from destruction,
Who Crowns you with lovingkindness and tender mercies,
Who satisfies your mouth with good things,
So that your youth is renewed like the eagles"

6

"Be holy, for I am Holy.
I am the Lord your God."

Leviticus 10:3,

> "By those who come near Me, I must be regarded as holy;
> And before all the people, I must be glorified."

6.1 More than just a command.

After listening to Pastor Benny Hinn's teachings on Spiritual warfare and demonology, I became hungry for more of his teachings. I spent nights tuning in to his teachings and conferences on YouTube, as well as to his "This is Your Day" broadcasts on his ministry website. During that season, he shared of how he had always made it a point to read the entire bible, at least twice a year. He encouraged his "precious people" to do the same. He said that God reveals deep secrets to those who wait on Him and search for Him. In the course of reading the bible many times over, Pastor Benny said that God began revealing to him secrets, hidden in many places in the bible that would have not been revealed to him, had he read the bible only once, or even twice.

Nothing occurred to me at first, until the third time when I tuned in to his "This is Your Day" broadcast as usual. Toward the end of that broadcast,

Pastor Benny suddenly spoke in the most serious tone, his finger pointing at "you, watching me now, start reading your bible today!" With a stern face (almost frowning), he said, "You never know what God wants to speak to you about!" The Holy Spirit immediately quickened to me to start reading the entire bible, from Genesis, all the way to Revelations. To be honest, I've never read the entire bible, even though I've been to a Bible College. I only studied, but not read, what was required, for the sake of writing essays and sitting for exams.

That night, I told the Lord that He had spoken, and that I will set my mind on reading the entire bible starting that weekend. As I make plans, I decided that, instead of reading the bible in my little room, I would go to a coastal village, find a quiet spot facing the sea, and spend the entire Saturday, and Sunday afternoon, just reading quietly together with the Holy Spirit. I began to embark on that journey, armed with a haversack filled with a can of mosquito repellent, a 1.2 litters water bottle, a box of tissue, a face towel, a hat, an umbrella, some snacks, and, of course, my New King James Bible.

It took me five months to finish reading the entire bible, a feat which I proudly gave myself a pat on the back. I felt refreshed and ministered to at different places in the bible, although I had not had any secrets revealed to me from the Lord. I sang songs that I know of along with David in the book of Psalms. Happy with my achievement, I put my bible aside, put Pastor Benny Hinn's teachings and ministry aside, as I became distracted with year-end festivities.

The following year, the Holy Spirit told me to read the bible again. As I was occupied with new developments that came up, I could not set aside my entire weekends as I did before. The weather was also no longer conducive for me to spend my time reading the bible at the coastal village. I grabbed whatever time I could get, and read as much as I could. I resumed with Pastor Benny Hinn's ministry at night, sometimes following his worship service, at other times listening to his teachings. Towards the end of that year, I managed to finish reading the Old Testament. I told the Lord that I would continue with the New Testament beginning the following year.

It was not to be so. The Holy Spirit told me to read the Old Testament again. When I came to the book of Leviticus, something suddenly occurred to me. I asked the Holy Spirit, why was it that the Lord had to keep repeating and reminding the children of Israel, over and over again, throughout the entire book, to be holy, because He is their God, and He is holy, and they must therefore sanctify themselves. Could He not just say it once, and punished those who defied Him as their God, defiled His holiness, and broke His commands?

The Holy Spirit told me that it was more than just a command. Behind that command was also a plea, a plea for His children to live a holy life, and to acknowledge Him alone as their God, because He created them in His image, in His likeness. He was pleading for them to live in His image because He loved them. It broke His heart to see His children stray away from Him and defile His image. That revelation by the Holy Spirit broke me to tears. I went on my knees immediately, and pledge my love to Him as my one and only God, and worshipped and praised Him.

Even as I write this, tears are welling in my eyes. As I picked myself up and began reading Leviticus again, the Holy Spirit told me to take note of these:

6.2 The steps of a good man are ordered by the Lord

> Leviticus 10:10, "that you may distinguish between holy and unholy, and between unclean and clean."

As God's redeemed children, set apart to live a holy life on this earth, let our steps be ordered by the Lord. As David puts it in Psalms 37:23-24; 27-29,

> "The steps of a good man are ordered by the Lord,
>   And He delights in His way – vs 23
> "Though he fall, he shall not be utterly cast down;

For the LORD upholds him with His hand – vs 24

Depart from evil, and do good;

And dwell forevermore – vs 27

For the LORD loves justice,

And does not forsake His saints;

They are preserved forever,

But the descendants of the wicked shall be cut off – vs 28

The righteous shall inherit the land,

And dwell in it forever" – vs 29.

The Lord God is speaking to us as His children to be holy, for He is holy. The Lord God is also speaking to us as His royal priesthood, to crucify and sanctify our flesh each day, even as He has sanctified our spirit man through the blood of Jesus Christ shed on the Cross for us.

6.3 Present your bodies a living sacrifice, holy, acceptable to God.

➤ Leviticus 11:44, "For I am the Lord your God. You shall therefore consecrate yourselves, and you shall be holy; for I am holy."

In Romans 12:1-2, Paul exhorted the Christians with this:

"I beseech you therefore, brethren, by the mercies of God,

That you present your bodies a living sacrifice,

Holy, acceptable to God,

Which is your reasonable service" "And do

not be conformed to this world,

But be transformed by the renewing

Of your mind,

That you may prove

What is that good and acceptable and

Perfect will of God"

We must make a conscientious effort every day to walk in the light of God's Word, to be able to discern between what's holy and unholy, clean and unclean, and to compare the world's wisdom with the wisdom of God. We ask the Holy Spirit to help us along the way, instead of stumbling along with the ways of the world.

6.4 Do not oppress each other

➤ Leviticus 25:17, "Therefore, you shall not oppress one another, but you shall fear your God; for I am the Lord your God."

Paul says in Romans 12:9-10,

> "Let love be without hypocrisy. Abhor what
> is evil. Cling to what is good"
> "Be kindly affectionate to one another with brotherly love,
> In honour giving preference to one another"

We need to be careful not to take things into our own hands, or make overbearing decisions that oppresses those we are biased against, for whatever reasons. Look at the strength instead of the weaknesses of the average believer. Even the "high-and-mighty" have their weaknesses.

6.5 Walk circumspectly

➤ Leviticus 26:13, "I am the Lord your God, who brought you out of the land of Egypt, that you should not be their slaves"

As God's children, we need to make a conscientious effort each day, to walk circumspectly in His image. We are no longer slaves to our flesh, as Jesus Christ has redeemed our sins at the Cross. We become dead to sin, and alive to God, as Paul says in Romans 6:6,

> "Knowing this, that our old man was crucified with
> Him, that the body of sin might be done away with,
> that we should no longer be slaves to sin."

In 2 Corinthians 5:17, Paul says "Therefore, if anyone is in Christ, he is a new creation; old things have passed away; behold, all things have become new."

With the Holy Spirit as our companion, we begin to put on the character of the new man, and set our minds on things above. In Colossians 3:10, Paul explained that the mind of the new man "is renewed in knowledge according to the image of Him who created him." As God's elect, "holy and beloved," we partner with the Holy Spirit in forgiving each other, and putting on "tender mercies, kindness, humility, meekness, longsuffering," (vs 12), and above all, "put on love, which is the bond of perfection" (vs 14).

As we begin to read the bible and internalise the Word of God in our hearts, our souls, and in our minds, we will also begin to find the trappings and enticement of this world repulsive to our new man. As the Holy Spirit begins to reveal the Glory of our Lord Jesus Christ in our spirits as a witness to His truth, His beauty, His splendour, His loveliness, His holiness, His purity, His righteousness, His glory, we can only stand in awe and wonder.

Press on! Be overcomers!

7.1 Set your eyes on the crown

Philippians 3:14, "I press toward the goal for the prize of the upward call of God in Christ Jesus."

Revelations 21:7-8,

> "He who overcomes shall inherit all things, and I will be his
> God and he shall be My son. But the cowardly, unbelieving,
> abominable, murderers, sexually immoral, sorcerers, idolaters,
> and all liars shall have their part in the lake which burns
> with fire and brimstone, which is the second death."

Have you by now set your eyes on the crown you want the Lord Jesus Christ to put on your head when He comes to bring you into His Glorious kingdom? Let's press on then towards the high calling of our faithful and loving God, our Abba Father! Let's cling tenaciously to our faith in the Lord Jesus Christ! Never, NEVER, NEVER let go of Him, no matter what happens all around us! No matter how the cowardly devil tries to instil fear in us, or discourage us from believing in the Almighty God! Cling tenaciously to our Lord Jesus Christ! Cling to Him! Start reading the bible TODAY! Let the Word of God be your staple spiritual food for your heart, your soul, and your mind!

7.2 Do not lose heart

2 Corinthians 4:16-18:

> "Therefore we do not lose heart. Even though
> our outward man is perishing,
> yet the inward man is being renewed day by day.
> For our light affliction, which is but for a moment, is working
> for us a far more exceeding and eternal weight of glory,
> While we do not look at the things which are seen, but at the
> things which are not seen. For the things which are seen are
> temporary, but the things which are not seen are eternal."

Hebrews 10:36-38,

> "For you have need of endurance, so that after you have
> done the will of God, you may receive the promise:
> 'For yet a little while,
> And He who is coming will come and not tarry.
> Now the just shall live by faith;
> But if anyone draws back,
> My soul has no pleasure in him.'

Press on, my fellow believers. Sceptics may laugh at you and ridicule your faith, and tell you to stop dreaming and "come down to earth", or atheists question your faith with their own wise philosophies. I have seen people who grew up loving and serving the Lord, suddenly becoming cold in their faith. They started to quote from great philosophers whom they read and learn about when they entered university. It is really sad to see them stray away from their faith so easily. But we can pray for them to turn back to Jesus.

7.3 The Glory and Lifter of my head - Psalm 3:3

> "But YOU, O LORD, are a shield for me,
> My glory and the ONE who lifts up my head;

I cried to the LORD with my voice,
And He heard me from His holy hill."

The Lord makes all things beautiful in His time to all those who cry to Him in their weak and helpless state. Our enemies may seem to triumph at that moment when they judge and decide that we are way below their glorious self. They may gang up against us and treat us harshly, hurl unkind and hurting words at us, and distance themselves from us. But the Lord, who loves us unconditionally, will lift our heads, exalts us, and prepare a table in the presence of our enemies, in due time. He resists the proud, but gives grace to the humble. So keep look up to the gracious Lord Jesus, and He will lift us up.

7.4 Declaration of faith

Let's declare together with David in Psalm 27:1, 4, 6, 13, 14,

"The Lord is my light and my salvation;
Whom shall I fear?
The Lord is the strength of my life;
Of whom shall I be afraid?

One thing I have desired of the LORD,
That will I seek:
That I may dwell in the house of the LORD
All the days of my life,
To behold the beauty of the LORD,
And to inquire in His temple;

And now my head shall be lifted up
Above my enemies all around me;
Therefore I will offer sacrifices of joy
In His tabernacle;
I will sing, yes, I will sing
Praises to the LORD!

I would have lost heart, unless I had believed
That I would see the goodness of the LORD
In the land of the living;

Wait on the LORD;
Be of good courage,
And He shall strengthen your heart;
Wait, I say, on the LORD!

The Lord will reward all those who wait patiently for His second coming. There will definitely be hard times and trying moments along the way, but those are to test our determination in clinging on tenaciously to our faith in Him, and His promises for each of us. He will fulfil His promises for us when He sees us always running to Him in our weaknesses, even as we struggle with having to face people who are mean to us.

Let's declare together with Paul in Romans 8:35-39:

"Who shall separate us from the love of Christ?
Shall tribulation, or distress, or persecution, or
famine, or nakedness, or peril, or sword?
As it is written: "For Your sake we are killed all day long;
We are accounted as sheep for the slaughter."
"Yet in all these things we are more than CONQUERORS
through HIM WHO LOVED US.
For I am persuaded that neither death nor life, nor angels nor
principalities nor powers, nor things present nor things to come,
Nor height nor depth, nor any other created thing, shall be able to
separate us from the love of God which is in Christ Jesus our Lord."

If God is for us, who can be against us? It doesn't matter if the "high-and-mighty" ignores us completely when we share what the Holy Spirit inspires us to share. God resist the proud, but chooses the foolish, weak things of the world to confound the wise (1 Corinthians 1:27). Who are they to shake our faith by doubting if we had really "heard" from the Lord? Who are they to think that God speaks only to certain ones and not to the average believer? The closer we walk with God, the more we attract people who have already harboured jealousy in their hearts without even them knowing that they are having that problem. We need not react badly to their attack. We stay away from them, and pray for them. Even if we can't reconcile with them, we still pray for them. It is good for our spiritual well-being, and we will not fall away from our walk and faith in God all too easily because of the "high-and-mighty".

Be filled with the Holy Spirit and walk in His Spirit instead of in the flesh, as Paul says in Galatians 5:22-23,

"But the fruit of the Spirit is love, joy, peace, longsuffering, kindness, goodness, faithfulness, gentleness, self-control. Against such there is no law."

Let's keep our eyes on Jesus and look forward to His coming, which is soon, and very soon. As the Lord Jesus declares in the last chapter of the book of Revelation 22:12-13,

> "And behold, I am coming quickly, and My reward is
> with Me, to give to everyone according to his work.
> "I am the Alpha and the Omega, the Beginning
> and the End, the First and the Last."

AMEN and AMEN!

Conclusion

CONGRATULATIONS! You have defeated the devil by reading this book to the end. It is challenging, but you made it! Hey, the end of this book is your beginning, really. It is the beginning of your journey toward receiving your crown as you get ready for the coming of the Glory of our Lord Jesus Christ! Hallelujah! Start reading the bible today! Draw close, and I mean, really close, to the Lord. Search the scriptures and let the Spirit of the Lord reveal deep secrets about Him to you personally. It is really precious and priceless to hear Him whisper His treasures into your heart as you seek after Him diligently with all your heart, with all your soul, and with all your mind! Amen and Amen! Meditate on the prayer of our Lord Jesus Christ in Mathew 11:27-30.

If you are a new believer and has not attended a church, go find one that moves in the power of the Holy Spirit, and one that demonstrates the love, grace, and mercies of God without being caught by religiosity and legalism, for "the letter kills, but the Spirit gives life" (2 Corinthians 3:6).

If you are already attending a church, make every effort to walk in the love, light, and wisdom of our Lord Jesus Christ, and be filled with the Spirit, "speaking to one another in psalms and hymns and spiritual songs, singing and making melody in your heart to the Lord, giving thanks always for all things to God the Father in the name of our Lord Jesus Christ" (Ephesians 5:19-20).

My prayer is for you, my fellow Christian, to begin to enjoy a very deep fellowship with the Lord Jesus Christ, with Abba Father, and with the Holy Spirit, every day! You will never be the same again when the Holy Spirit touches your heart! When you have tasted of His love, goodness and mercy, you will want to pass on His Spirit of Love to others! The Crown of Rejoicing and the Crown of Glory are yours when you share the love of Abba Father, the salvation work of Christ, and the Holy Spirit to others. What a great day it will be to see your loved ones, your friends, and those you bring to Christ, entering together with you into His Glorious Kingdom! For "as many as received Him, to them He gave the right to become children of God, to those who believe in His name" – John 1:12.

E-References

Chapter 2: The Five Crowns in the Bible
http://www.generationword.com/notes_for_notesbooks_pg/eternal_rewards_crowns_files/psoft.masonry(1).htm
http://www.g-m-a-g.com/message5.htm
http://biblehub.com/2_timothy/4-8.htm

Printed in the United States
By Bookmasters